GREGORY J. LAUGHERY

LIVING SPIRITUAL RHYTHMS

BOOK 1

destinée

Published by Destinée Media, www.destineemedia.com
SECOND EDITION
Book formatting by Robynn Sims and Eric Reynolds
Cover design by Eric Reynolds
Copy editing by Robynn Sims

ISBN 978-1-938367-13-7

CONTENTS

acknowledgements

I am deeply grateful to Robynn Sims for her help with this book. In every way, she has made the book much better by far, than it was to begin with.

I owe a debt of gratitude to Eric Reynolds who always gave gracious and skilled assistance. He creatively accomplished all he was asked to do and plenty more.

Were it not for the staff, helpers, students, guest speakers, authors, poets, and blog commentators, who in some sense all make up the Swiss L'Abri community, there would be little to write.

Un grand Merci goes to each and every one.

foreword

Often we find ourselves questioning why our lives do not reflect what we believe. If we believe that Jesus was who he said he was, then why are we not living out the compassionate calling that he gave us? In a time when the words "daily devotional" mean little more than reading a single verse of the Bible attached to a simplistic personal application for the day, an indulgence all too frequently far removed from the totality of what God intends, Dr. Gregory J. Laughery offers us a fresh perspective. By intertwining language that is both provocative and engaging, he encourages us to use our imaginations and to begin to open our minds and our hearts to new ways of seeing, being, and living for the sake of the gospel, which truly is good news for all. As we do so, the hope is that these new ways of viewing the world, culture, Scripture, God, the church, and redemption will draw us back to the story that is of old—the story of God's love and truth. May you find yourself challenged and refreshed by Dr. Laughery's reflections, which are truly embodied in one who lives out his spirituality in humility and grace day after day.

Robynn Sims
Swiss L'Abri

Dear Reader,

Faced with so many false options and outlooks today, sunrise and sunset seem to close us into diminishing possibilities for finding realistic and true spiritual rhythms of life. The purpose of this book is to open up new horizons for living spirituality; for being in community with God, through Jesus Christ, in the power of the Spirit, and for living this intimate and profound reality out into the world in redemptive and loving ways.

Living Spiritual Rhythms for Today has its focus on "living" as both verb and adjective. These rhythms therefore are living in the sense that they come out of my experience of being in community with God, and they are offered to you to be lived in an adventurous dynamic sense that I hope resonates with your own spiritual journey.

I want to extend to you dear reader, a warm invitation to deeply engage with this text. Keep it at hand, in your backpack or by your bedside, on a walk in the mountains or through the city. Meditate on the words, answer the questions, and take notes in the blank spaces and pages or in the margins. I've intentionally left plenty of room here for your responses and reflections. As you ponder the call to love and truth in this book, it is crucial to realize that we don't just read texts; they read us, as well. The goal of an encounter with this text is not to casually read through it, but to be read by it. In attentive reading and being read, there is an important moment of critical surrender that leads on to an appropriating of that which is not our own. Reading wisely opens us up to new possibilities. Being read challenges our hearts and minds, shapes our characters and identities, and changes our spiritualities and lives.

To be sure, we desperately need to be read by the text if we are to become better readers, and being better readers will help us discover more about spiritual rhythms of life for today.

Memories

Darkness shrouds that long lost valley
Billowing grey blinds vision of fleeting sky

Crevices and curvatures
Swallowing contours of obscurity
Dreams of hoping, seeing

To the Heavens cries earth
Open a deep and lasting illumination
Remembering, forgetting

Moon songs glowing at dusk
Flowing from a cherished sun lost
Fading recollection of sight
Waiting for light

economy of gift

In a world where we experience the "economy of exchange"
on a daily basis,
from our bank accounts
to our relationships,
viewing the love we offer to others through the lens of the "economy of gift" will radically alter the way we give and receive. To love the other with expectations attached is not love; it is exchange. This goes something like: If you do this for me, then I'll do that for you. Let us rather seek to offer our love as a gift, and as we do so to recognize that we are operating within a **new economy** that reverses and challenges our notions of love and sets us on the path to life.

Loving someone who loves you is easy love. Loving someone who doesn't love you is "hard love." Disciples of Jesus are to "hard love" those who don't love them. In spite of their broken, insufficient, and inadequate ways, disciples' love is nevertheless to be an active, seeking, and compassionate love, grounded in following God, who is love.

One of the greatest gifts of God is **excess.** *We never come to the end of God, the love of God, creation, others, or ourselves. To explore this living excess is far from an auto-pilot mechanism, and closer to an imaginative seeking to understand the past, present, and future well. Walking with God, the other, and ourselves in creation is a humble endeavor and a communal enterprise founded on love.*

From The Prelude, Book XII, 1850
by William Wordsworth

Long time have human ignorance and guilt
Detained us, on what spectacles of woe
Compelled to look, and inwardly oppressed
With sorrow, disappointment, vexing thoughts,
Confusion of the judgment, zeal decayed,
And lastly, utter loss of hope itself
And things to hope for! Not with these began
Our song, and not with these our song must end.

Theirs is the language of the heavens, the power,
The thought, the image, and the silent joy,
Words are but under-agents in their souls;
When they are grasping with their greatest strength,
They do not breathe among them: this I speak
In gratitude to God, Who feeds our hearts
For his own service; knoweth us, loveth us,
When we are unregarded by the world.

Jesus gives us some powerful words in Luke 6: *"But I tell you who listen: Love your enemies, do good to those who hate you, bless those who curse you, pray for those who mistreat you."*

Tangible expressions of grace and love are crucial markers for the Christian community and for others to come to know Christ through it. Our acts of love or lovelessness have a massive power to redemptively embrace or ungraciously reject others. To see ourselves rightly is to recognize that we are seen by God, who calls us to missionally testify to his love in a broken and hurting world. How can being rightly seen translate into love expressed?

"I was told I was loved," someone once conveyed to me. "My parents said they loved me and that's why they demanded my full attention. And I believed this was true." **Do you think this is love?**

Love

Paul's words in chapter 13 of his first letter to the Corinthians ***scream*** out, but so often it seems we are ***deaf***. Let's ask God to help change that.

Listen, hear, and act:

"Love is patient,
love is kind. It does not envy, *it does not boast,*
it is not proud.
It is not rude,
it is not self-seeking,
it is not easily angered,
it keeps no record of wrongs.
Love does not delight in evil but
rejoices with the truth.
It always protects,
always trusts,
always hopes, and
always perseveres."

We may think we know very well what love is until someone asks us: What is love?

Why does the

"economy of exchange"

reign over that of the

"economy of gift"

in so many of our churches and relationships?

Are we afraid of something?

Yes.

Does a spirit of fear control too much of our lives?

Yes.

Fear sweeps over us like pelting sheets of driving rain and floods our minds and hearts. What we fear therefore becomes the center of who we are.

Thoughts?

Break on through, Lord. Let the current of your love transform our hearts and minds so that we might be gracious representatives of Christ in the church and in the world.

Hospitality

It is indeed wonderfully exciting to offer hospitality and shelter in the midst of life's chaos, bewilderment, and uncertainty. Hospitality and home-sharing are deep expressions of Christian spirituality. Amazing that in a world of the fake and counterfeit what's real continues to happen again and again. Lamentably, many today find their identities in the hollow promises of media, consumerism, and making it up as they go along. Christians have more to offer. We are to invite these precious people into the festive adventure of seeking truth, spiritual direction, meaning and purpose in life, credibility, and authenticity. As we extend hospitality to others, let's be grateful that God hospitably meets us all in a diversity of ways on the journey.

Being in community with God and each other is **a joy and a privilege.** In seeking to do the Lord's work in the Lord's way, the apostle Paul challenges us Christians to have a deep unity amongst ourselves as we follow Christ, so that we might glorify God with one heart and one voice. To accept one another as brother and sister then, just as Christ has accepted us, will ultimately be pleasing to God, and offer a striking testimony to his love.

Lord, help us to welcome strangers, and to break down any barriers that still haunt us. Keep us open to and aware of the truth that you call and address people from every tribe, every nation, and every tongue. May hospitality overflow from our hearts out into the lonely streets, so that charity abounds to those in need.

Giving Sacrifice

Many Christians today have lost a sense of sacrifice. We must move away from being doped on our culture of gluttony: Money, possessions, and consumerism—and move towards the living God and his love. Getting everything that everyone else does is so ingrained in the fiber of our lives that we have become delirious, shrouded in darkness, and we are losing our way. By contrast, sacrificially giving to others in love and mercy illumines the path, and we begin to understand what it means to follow Christ.

As we work together doing the Lord's work in the Lord's way, we can participate in reversing the flow of the cultural force of treating others as a means to an end. People are not a means to an end. They are human beings, precious to God and are therefore to be respected, nurtured, and loved.

Do you think it is easier to **judge** *than to* **love?**

We may have heard that God will fulfill all our longings and needs. Do you believe it? I don't, because God is a Creator who has expressly given us each other and a world that are meant to be integral parts of fulfilling these longings and needs. After all, in the Genesis narrative, God says that it's not good for man to be alone. If God had intended to fulfill all our longings and needs, there would have been no reason to say "it is not good....".

growing trust

Sometimes we sense a loss of contact with

God.

We grope around in darkness longing for light
and wander through the wilderness
thirsting for a cup of water.
When this happens, we need to cling to God,
cling to his promises,
to the truth that we are not on our own,
and to the reality that we have a destiny of
being transformed into the image of Christ.
Struggling to find the way in the desert is no easy task.

God seems distant,

yet we know he's there. During these times we plead:

Oh God,

offer us cold refreshing cups of water to sustain us,
and encourage a growing trust that will provide strength
to continue on until we, once more,
intimately meet you again.

May our desire for God's substantial healing be greater than our fear of failure. Let's live in the hope of Christ's second coming and not be presently defeated by that which seems insurmountable.

The Bible frequently speaks of hope.

What is it?

Breaking through the darkness to the other side and into the glow of light that God provides in Christ is a profound experience of love and grace.

As we forge through the difficult times in our own lives,
a shadow is always there beckoning us towards the hope of the illuminated path ahead.

Giving Thanks

As the Apostle Paul so eloquently puts it:
I give thanks to God always for you because of the grace of God that has been given you in Christ Jesus, for in every way you have been enriched in him, in all speech and knowledge, just as the testimony of Christ was confirmed in you - so that you are not lacking in any spiritual gift, as you wait for the revealing of Jesus Christ. He will also strengthen you to the end so that you may be blameless on the day of our Lord Jesus Christ. God is faithful; by him you were called into fellowship with his son, Jesus Christ our Lord.

(1 Corinthians 1:4-9)

The perpetual cycle of sin can diminish in our lives
by
the grace of God,
the revelation of his word,
the gift of the Holy Spirit.
In our own sanctified and redemptive being
and becoming like Christ, there can be a
renewal in every present situation—self to God,
self to self,
self to other,
self to world.

Release us, oh Lord, from the power of sin that chains us in the darkness, and bring us into your liberating light, so that we might live anew for the sake of Jesus.

Being grace-filled is receiving and giving a gift.
Forgiveness: Unconditional or Conditional?

On the basis of the finished work of Christ, God forgives all.
That is, God establishes forgiveness unconditionally.
Access to God's forgiveness, however, is conditional in that
for us it can only be received through our confession of sin
and our request that God grant us this forgiveness.

Do you think there should be a connection between forgiveness and forgetting?

Forgiveness is not a mechanism,
but an embodied way of life
connected to being in community with God.
To forgive is to forgive as we've been forgiven.
Take a risk—break on through to the other side
far away from guilt and condemnation and

rejoice in release.

Celebrate the reality that our words and deeds are
being performed on the stage of the Kingdom of
God, which is founded upon and centered in
Jesus Christ.

What is forgiveness? Does it refer to release?

Grace

has been misplaced. Everything seems to be focused on negotiation. Surpassing notions of exchange or deal making however, is the directedness of God for our lives.

There are plenty of ungracious attitudes around. We all make mistakes, sin, and are in need of redemption. Thank God for Christ. Embrace grace and then give it away in generosity. God's grace comes to us superabundantly and freely. Let's offer it to others in overflowing joy.

May the

power

of the

Holy Spirit

deeply indwell us
individually and in community
as we follow the missional trajectory
of witnessing to the Christ to the ends of the earth.

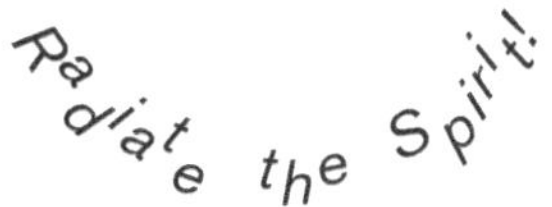

The Holy Spirit is not some vague impersonal force or energy, or a guide without a map merely doing his own thing. In contrast, he is a personal agent whose actions are in harmony with the Father and the Son, and who therefore is a capable and loving guide in that he points us back to them, to the map of Scripture, and how to live as we move towards our destination of imaging Christ. Clearly, the Spirit and the map are to work together. Map reading is not a given, but a challenge which requires growing levels of competence and hearing the Spirit. The Spirit glorifies the risen Christ, acting as his very presence, illuminating the map in accordance with the loving directions that unfold for followers of Christ Jesus.

—From Living Spirituality: Illuminating the Path

Remember we're not alone. As we celebrate Pentecost each year, we can be thankful that the Holy Spirit was poured out and that he guides and directs our lives as the presence of Christ with us, until the end of the age.

May we be thankful that we have received the gift of the Holy Spirit. The biblical Holy Spirit is not some impersonal force or vague natural phenomenon, but the Spirit of God and of Christ. It is this Spirit who illuminates the path to life and who will be with us until the end of the age.

living in tension

There is a tension between being and doing.

Often we are confronted with this question, especially in the West, "What do you do?" The implication is that who we are is based in what we do as work; therefore our identities may be wrapped tightly in our occupations and doings.

We are more.

Charles Taylor in Ethics of Authenticity, 17, expounds on the way that what we do has infiltrated who we are:

"What we need to explain is what is peculiar to our time. It's not just that people sacrifice their love relationships and the care of their children, to pursue careers. ***The point is that today many people feel called to do this, feel they ought to do this, feel their lives would be somehow wasted or unfulfilled if they didn't do it.****" Let us remember what we are called to in this context: To live out spirituality that is consistent with the teachings of Jesus. This living spirituality is rooted in who we are as his followers and then in what we do as a result of this reality.*

Feeling sad much of the time can happen to us.
Sometimes, in these circumstances,
there is a desire to lash out and
destroy even the good
that may be evident.

During these hard periods,
we need to remember that God is
trustworthy and that we can seek to create
and not destroy. Life is lived moment by moment;
change and transformation, *through the mercy of God,*

are real possibilities.

Ever been depressed?

Why do you think depression is so widespread today?

I recently read

about a church

that became

a coffee bar.

The pastor

confessed that

people liked

the espressos,

frappes, and

pastries better

than the

ministry.

He reckoned

that God

was telling

the church to

focus on its

strengths –

being relevant

means giving

the people

what they want:

Coffee drinks

and chocolate-

filled donuts.

Why are

churches

turning into

coffee houses,

apartment

buildings, and

art museums?

To be living on the borders, the edge, brings a variety of questions to mind. Here's one for you:

Where are Christians to situate themselves in a culture gone mad with consumerism?

The folly of "shopping" tears into the very fabric of who we are and seeks to assure us that everything will be okay if we consume. Shop to our heart's delight is the evangelistic message for today. Our hope, as some would have it, is in the eternal gift of acquisition. Why, we're even mediatized to devour each other.

And then another question:

Do you find there's a problem with the mission of consumerism and the impact it is having on the church?

Lamentably, the founding stories of our faith are so often entombed in church buildings that lack the presence of God, or in electronic boxes that perpetrate a mindless faith in consumerism. By contrast, the subversive and radical power of the mission, ministry, and person of Jesus illumines the path towards authenticity. Cherish the gospels, read them diligently, appreciate their relation and distinction, and above all, live their truth in *love.*

Christians devote a tremendous amount of time and energy in attempting to

In my view, this is a utopian misinterpretation of living spirituality and not the direction God has for us. To be in tension is to be in-between. And being in-between corresponds to the theological marker of the Kingdom of God, to life in the world, and to who we are as creatures of God.

As Jesus is now absent and the New Covenant not yet complete, ***how are we to live in-between lives in the inadequacy of the present?***

Lord, help us to give up not praying. As with many addictions that we put false hope in – even though we tend to know that it is false hope and we can't quit and return to it again and again, not praying is tough to stop doing. We ask that we would be released to pray more frequently and fervently. Amen.

Living Perceptively

There's so much deception around.
Darkness masquerades as light, lies as truth and the unreal as real. Foreign gods, foreign spirits, and foreign gospels invade and threaten to dismantle the one true gospel, centered in the crucified and risen One.
And lamentably, much of this takes place in our churches. In our own day, God, spirit, and gospel can mean anything if they are not carefully defined and their sense and referent traced out with dynamic biblical research and study. Discernment and wisdom are crucial for the Christian life, especially today.
In all things, oh God, please grant us these insights for the sake of the gospel and Jesus Christ our Lord.

What might emerging spirituality look like for the church?

Living life on earth is sometimes like being lost in thick billows of fog. We see very little of what's ahead or behind and feel closed in. As we are forced to slowly and carefully inch our way along, let's hope to learn more of the deep truth of trusting the Author of our world and our salvation.

The failure of the self contained centered self, the "I" of high modernity, has all too often translated into the entrapped, reduced, de-centered self, the "ZERO" of low postmodernity. While clearing debris away from ourselves is an essential priority and a continual process of same and change, we begin to realize the glaring necessity is to find a "real" self **in the midst** of the wreckage. Unfortunately, our legitimate fears of being deceived may lead us into further deceptions in an embrace of the "I" or the "ZERO", though instead our trajectory towards protection is to turn to Christian revelation and faith, which offer us a credible way through to a re-centered and reconstituted self beyond the arrogant "I" or the imprisoned "ZERO".

Lord God, our hearts are so often cluttered with debris. There's so much rubble that needs to be rearranged and piles of refuse that should be thrown out. Help us start the process of heart transformation and renewal. We sometimes assume that if we just had more time, money, and possessions, or if we looked better, were more talented and wise, the condition of our hearts would improve. This is simply not true. Redeem and cleanse us, Lord God, so that we might more truly seek after you and your kingdom with a renewed and pure heart.

Presumption & Despair | Imaginative presumption or despair plays a massive role in our contexts. Culturally speaking there's a Seinfeld god, an absent god, an image god, a nature god, an internet god, a republican or democrat god, or a powerless god, to mention just a few of the representations of the gods of culture that can lead to despair. More specifically, in Christian circles, we often find an overdose of presumption. Some Christians imagine that they know exactly what God is doing, and that through the Spirit God speaks directly to them. A Christian once told me that he could be perfect in this life because the Spirit had assured him that was the case. Another time a believer insisted that a verse in Isaiah was written explicitly for her. Misleading fictions like these tend to be prominent today, but such presumption has more to do with self-centeredness than it does truly knowing, imaginatively and otherwise, the living God.

In today's world of

Post–Everything,

how are you surviving?

Shaming

*Tombstones
adorn the
church inside and
out. Release us, oh
God, from this graveyard
of tears. Melody sent me an
e-mail asking how to cope with
the shaming that goes on in her more
traditionally-minded church. Every time she
comments about the teaching in her church, she's
made to feel sub-human, yet she has excellent points to
make. Now experiencing a deep sense of shame in even
asking questions, she is suffering scorn from those who are
idiotically ignorant concerning her gifts and spiritual starvation.
Here's what makes it more difficult: She has nowhere to turn.
Family and friends attend this church. Melody thinks she
has to stay. Why do you think there is
so much shaming going on in*

churches?

Conflict

I like these words from Samuel Taylor Coleridge's *What is Life?* Written around 1805.
He expresses conflict like this:

Resembles Life what once was held of Light,
Too ample in itself for human sight?
An absolute Self--an element ungrounded--
All, that we see, all colours of all shade
By encroach of darkness made?--
Is very life by consciousness unbounded?
And all the thoughts, pains, joys of mortal breath,
A war-embrace of wrestling Life and Death?

What's your fragrance?

To those entrusted with the gospel, mission is spreading the fragrance of Christ, both to those being saved and to those who are perishing – the fragrance of life and death.

The aroma of the former is like a scent that gets better and better, while the scent of the latter is like a stench that gets worse and worse.

Confidence without humility is arrogance.
Humility without confidence is relativism.

Remembering

Many today see the recounting of one's past as a manipulative battle between the victim and the victimizer. While it is not possible to recount total truth because we're situated in space and time, and we perceive things from our own contexts, does this mean that, "I remember," is merely equated with making it up as I go along? To call something true about the past in our culture, I think, has become more like creating a stimulating story that entertains, or is used to further certain purposes. Do you think this is the case? Would you say there is any place left today for "I remember…." making a claim to something that is sufficiently true?

From The Prelude, Book XIII, 1805
by William Wordsworth

Meanwhile, the Moon look'd down upon this shew
In single glory, and we stood, the mist
Touching our very feet; and from the shore
At a distance not the third part of a mile
Was a blue chasm; a fracture in the vapour,
A deep and gloomy breathing-place through which
Mounted the roar of waters, torrents, streams
Innumerable, roaring with one voice.
The universal spectacle throughout
Was shaped for admiration and delight,
Grand in itself alone, but in that breach
Through dark deep thoroughfare had Nature lodg'd
The Soul, the Imagination of the whole.

What seems a blow to the ego may help us find a better footing to live the life of faith and to trust God. A deflated ego can be a vibrant reminder that God should come first in our lives. When we put God first, we're on our way to being true selves, those who are being transformed into the image of the crucified and risen One.

Living spiritually is enhanced and enriched through the Psalms, and their frequent affirmations of and appeals to God's covenant loyalty. Many of these writings, however, may shock us with their realism. In the midst of our sometimes automatic pilot spirituality, where everything is supposedly bright and happy, some of the Psalms remind us that community with God and the path to life are far from straight forward. There is and will be brokenness, mystery, dark times, judgment, desperate searching, and much more. Though these circumstances frequently lead to illumination and new understanding, arriving there means going through—not taking a detour around—facets of spirituality that may not fit our desired schemes, notions, and expectations of God. The path may become difficult and the destination may seem far away, but God is faithful to lead us forward. The Psalms are ***a richly textured slice of life with God***, and they offer us revelatory insights into humanness and living spirituality.

—From Living Spirituality: Illuminating the Path.

Peddling the Gospel

Cunning words and clever speech have the powerful capacity to divert our attention from what is most central to us—sincere devotion to Christ. Whatever happened to the church proclaiming Christ, instead of a being a parody of cultural consumerism rooted in the art of rhetoric, which aims to give the consumer what they want and to reap the financial windfall connected to it? How much should one have to pay to have the true gospel preached to them?

To receive someone's words is a continual challenge of discernment, and we want to be alert and aware in order to receive with caution and clarity. The discernment of diversion necessitates a fine balance between trust and suspicion. Whom shall we trust? Whom shall we be suspicious of? When preaching Jesus becomes self-centered, when there's a spirit of pride, and when this supposed gospel counters that of the crucified Christ, we know the answer. Peddlers of this gospel, which cannot be the true gospel, will have the end that such actions deserve.

In Revelation 3:14-22, Christ wishes that the Christians in Laodicea were either hot or cold. It is often assumed that hot means "on fire for the Lord" or a full commitment, while cold means, "no fire for the Lord," or no commitment. If this is the case, the question we're faced with is why Christ would approve of no commitment at all? This doesn't make sense. Hot and cold are not to be taken as positive and negative descriptions, but both are positive in regard to what the church's actions should be. The problem is being lukewarm, which seems to identify all too many churches. We, like the Laodiceans, proclaim we're rich, but Christ says we're impoverished. True riches are spiritual, not found in material possessions, but in Christ himself.

Counterfeit forms of spirituality are often characterized by a hyper-subjectivity or hyper-objectivity, which have little or nothing to do with Christian truth or with the whole of life in God's world. It is essential to be aware of the proliferation of these popularized cultural manifestations that are anti-spirituality, and by contrast, to speak and live the truth in love, as we battle against the clutches of death.

May the grace of the Lord Jesus Christ be with you.

Sometimes we experience wilderness wanderings where God seems far, so far away. There is an acute sense of God's absence in our lives and we stumble along as if on our own. Meet us where we are, oh Lord, and bring us out and into the shelter of your promise that your presence is always with us. Help us to have a renewed trust that your mission to redeem the world includes us.

American Woes

Decline seems to characterize the once great **United States of America. Shocking expressions of** rampant consumerism and making what one can **off someone else's misfortune signal what's really** important for many: Profit. The current breakdown **of stable relationships and families is creating a** culture without a home. Many don't have any idea **where they're going or where they've just been. This** growing loss of contact with God as home: Providing **community, stability, trust, justice, and love means** that the real world has less and less impact on living **life. Surrounded by the sound bite superficiality of** politics and church, there's nowhere left to turn. Help. **We need to find our way home.**

From The Prelude, Book V, 1805
by William Wordsworth

Now this is hollow, 'tis a life of lies
From the beginning, and in lies must end
Forth bring him to the air of common sense,
And, fresh and shewy as it is, the Copse
Slips from us into powder. Vanity
That is his soul, there lives he, and there moves;
It is the soul of everything he seeks;
That gone, nothing is left which he can love.

Trust and Suspicion

There is a heavy emphasis on suspicion these days and rightly so. Suspicion is an important element of not being duped; no one wants to be duped. When people get burned once, they swear it will never happen again. This has left trust in a bad way. Trust, I've heard it said, has been maligned, manipulated, and discredited. Suspicion reigns and no one wants to trust anymore. But this is more a part of a grand illusion than it is true. Why? Suspicion is rooted in trust. That is, trust

precedes

suspicion

and

suspicion

requires

trust.

Otherwise, and let's face it, suspicion wouldn't exist and we would just say, "That's the way it is." But we don't. If this is true, it leads to several conclusions:

First, human beings cannot escape trust.

Second, the world we live in is a world that requires and gets trust.

Third, God as Creator and Redeemer calls us to be suspicious of certain claims, people, and things, while trusting in others.

And learning what to be suspicious of and what to trust is a life-long task of seeking to follow in the footsteps of Christ.

From The Prelude, Book VI, 1805
by William Wordsworth

In living Nature, I had there a guide
Which open'd frequently my eyes, else shut,
A standard which was usefully applied,
Even when unconsciously, to other things
Which less I understood. In general terms,
I was a better judge of thoughts than words,
Misled as to these latter, not alone
By common inexperience of youth
But by the trade in classic niceties,
Delusion to young Scholars incident
And old ones also, by that overpriz'd
And dangerous craft of picking phrases out
From languages that want the living voice
To make of them a nature to the heart,
To tell us what is passion, what is truth,
What reason, what simplicity and sense.

In the late twentieth and early twenty-first century, many Christians have moved in one of two directions: Embracing absolute arrogance or absolute humility. To be sure, both these expressions, in this form, are problematic. It is thoroughly bewildering that some Christians hold onto the ridiculous notion that they're right about everything, or that no one else is right about anything.

A better configuration would be something like

this: Confidence without humility is arrogance and humility without confidence is relativism. These two are in tensional dialogue, disallowing any absolute form of one, or the other. Living spirituality is tethered to dialogue, and dialogue s h a t t e r s these monologues of false absolutes.

Scripture deeply searches for ways to express the greatness of God, but words are unable to capture God's magnificent power and complexity. While words are significant and meaningful, God transcends and surpasses anything that could ever be said in words. The fullness of the mystery of God, however, has been revealed in Christ, yet the complete reality of Christ is known to only the personal divine being of God.

Tenacious obscurity sometimes plagues us and we're unable to see as clearly as we would like. Groping around for illumination saturates our thoughts and feelings, and there are no easy answers. We fear being Xcluded, alienated, and lost. Yet, living and working through the shadow of time is continually a challenge to find the light and to embrace it as we are able. *May the eyes of our hearts be illuminated, as we seek to know the love of Christ that surpasses knowledge.*

God has empowered us through his grace, through the gift of righteousness, and through a union with Christ to live in a new ways. This recognition carries with it a new allegiance, not to sin, but to God. It is this power that operates in living spirituality and enables us to live life toward God.

The enactment of this transfer of lordship is working its way to completion in our lives now, even in a moment-by-moment way. Just because it will only be complete in the future does not mean it is irrelevant or insignificant for living our present lives. We are alive to God in Christ.

From The Prelude, Book XI, 1805
by William Wordsworth

What then remained in such eclipse? what light
To guide or chear? The laws of things which lie
Beyond the reach of human will or power;
The life of nature, by the God of love
Inspired, celestial presence ever pure;
These left, the Soul of Youth must needs be rich,
Whatever else be lost, and these were mine,
Not a deaf echo, merely, of thought
Bewilder'd recollections, solitary,
But living sounds.

Christ is Lord of all of life now, and together we are part of God's unfolding drama of his mission to humanity and the world. May God help us to be living in the light of the return of Christ as it relates to present expectation and action towards social, political, and ethical change; for we await a redeemer who is renewing and will renew all things. Therefore, in the apostle Paul's terms, we are not to be conformed to this age, but be transformed by the renewing of our minds, so that we might discern God's will and offer ourselves as living sacrifices in doing it.

In a startling passage in Revelation 1:8, using the Greek alphabet, God now refers to himself with the first and last letters. He is the beginning and the end. No power is greater than his power. In spite of the difficult circumstances and devastating persecution, the Almighty himself professes his ultimate sovereign control of the end of history. This magnificent and reassuring title, Alpha and Omega, occurs ten times in the New Testament, and four of these references are in the Apocalypse.

We are in a triumphal procession and let's be grateful for the polyvalence of the imagery in 2 Corinthians 2:14. It stands for, I believe, both victory and humiliation, which are both part of the gospel mission and ministry. Humiliations can abound and result in rejection, yet God in Christ accepts us, and this leads us on to victory.

From Tintern Abbey, 1798
by William Wordsworth

... I cannot paint
What then I was. The sounding cataract
Haunted me like a passion; the tall rock,
The mountain, and the deep and gloomy wood,
Their colours and their forms, were then to me
An appetite; a feeling and a love,
That hath no need of remoter charm,
By thought supplies, nor any interest
Unborrowed from the eye. – That time is past,
And all its aching joys are no more,
And all its dizzy raptures. Not for this
Faint I, no mourn nor murmur; other gifts
Have followed; for such loss, I would believe,
Abundant recompense. For I have learned
To lock on nature, not as in the hour
Of thoughtless youth; but hearing oftentimes
The still, sad music of humanity ...

Praise God for who he is and for what he has done, is doing and will do - for his mission through creation, Israel and the Christ to renew and redeem humanity and the world.

Living Story | No one's story is fully written in the now. Don't get caught up in the eternal return of the present with the living dead. As children of God we're travelling on the journey to our destiny, which is to image Christ. If movement and transformation are not part of your theology, change it. Hope deserves—as does rapturous love—a startling embrace that enlivens our notion of being on the way in living our unfinished story.

From The Prelude, Book XII, 1805
by William Wordsworth

This is for the past, and things that may be view'd
Or fancied, in the obscurities of time.

We should neither be reading every event on the world's stage as end time's prophecy, nor should we be naïve. Interpreting the times calls for Christians to have minds of wisdom and hearts of patient endurance. We can continue to trust in both God's faithful working out of his purposes and the victory that believers already participate in because of the blood of the Lamb.

Throne theophanies in Scripture are visions of God enthroned. God is holy, almighty, and who was, is, and is to come. He lives forever and ever. He is worthy for he has created all things. Revelation 5 captures one of these awesome scenes. In this majestic scene there is assurance that those facing dire circumstances and life-threatening persecution can trust God. In a world that may seem to be out of control, in a world of suffering and death, God is there, moving history to its cataclysmic consummation.

God is the mystery of the world. What a wonder that we have in Scripture and nature the knowledge of God that we do. Praise God today for the gracious revelation that has been given to us, and may we act on what we have, as we await the fullness of the future.

From The Prelude, Book I, 1805
by William Wordsworth

Sometimes it suits me better to shape out
Some Tale from my own heart, more near akin
To my own passions and habitual thoughts,
Some variegated story, in the main
Lofty, with interchange of gentler things.
But deadening admonitions will succeed
And the whole beauteous Fabric seems to lack
Foundation, and, withal, appears throughout
Shadowy and unsubstantial. Then, last wish,
My last and favorite aspiration! then
I yearn towards some philosophic Song
Of Truth that cherishes our daily life;
With meditations passionate from deep
Recesses in heart, immortal verse
Thoughtfully fitted to the Orphean lyre;
But from this awful burthen I full soon
Take refuge, and beguile myself with trust
That mellower years will bring riper mind
And cleared insight. Thus from day to day
I live, a mockery of the brotherhood
Of vice and virtue, with no skill to part
Vague longing that is bred by want of power
From paramount impulse not be withstood,
A timourous capacity from prudence;
From circumspection, infinite delay.

We
are not to be
just sitting around waiting
for the lordship of Christ to come.
Christ is Lord of all of life now, and together
we are part of God's unfolding drama of a mission to
humanity and the world. Hope and longing
for justice are piercings that identify
us. May God help us to be
living in the light of the
return of Christ as
it relates to
present
expectation
and action
towards
social,
political,
and ethical
change, for
we await a
redeemer
who will
renew all
things.

(left intentionally blank for notes)

creational perspective

Environmental issues stir emotions on all sides of the political spectrum, and Christians find themselves immersed in the milieu of this controversial dialogue. Unfortunately, it seems as though Christians, in the West at least, have had a rather dubious history in this arena; we have either condemned the dialogue all together, or we have championed capitalistic ideals over anything "green." We are now at what seems to be a crucial crossroads for the Church in this postmodern world. Many seem to be wholeheartedly embracing everything "green" as a way of trying to atone for the sins of the past. Others still seem skeptical beyond reason that the environment matters at all. But amid this seeming shouting match of ideas, Christians must embrace this opportunity to both make amends for the past and lay a foundation for future dialogue. In humility, we must engage in this dialogue with the script of Scripture and creation as our guides. As we recognize that creation has been given as a gift by the Creator God, we must make choices that reflect our desire for responsible stewardship. Within our dialogue, our perspective brings with it the beautiful aspect of redemption. As we offer this hopeful perspective, we celebrate that this world is not all there is—that God has promised to redeem creation. This is the hope that we have that should spur us on to join in creational renewal that is deeply connected to the cross of Christ. Jesus' sacrifice not only began the redeeming work for humanity, but also the redeeming work for creation, as well. To live as followers of the crucified and risen One, we must recognize the fullness of the bringing things to rights both for humanity and for creation.

From The Prelude, Book VII, 1805
by William Wordsworth

Attention comes
And comprehensiveness and memory,
From early converse with the works of God
Among all regions; chiefly where appear
Most obviously simplicity and power.
The mountain's outline and its steady form
Gives a pure grandeur, and its presence shapes
The measure and the prospect of the soul
To majesty; such virtue have the forms
Perennial of the ancient hills; nor less
The changeful language of their countenances
Gives movement to the thoughts, and multitude,
With order and relation.

Remembering the Creator and Creation

In the founding narrative of beginnings in Genesis, God is depicted as the mighty Creator who takes on the role of the great actor in time and story. On this register, the cosmic revelatory drama of God speaking, acting, and proclaiming is to be considered as sculpting in time. Portrayed as revealing in, through, and beyond time, the Genesis God chisels out the contours of nature, humanity, and story, and vanquishes all counterfeit claims to creational authority concerning the theodrama of creation. Understood in these terms, narrative time in Genesis becomes a literary device that negotiates a temporal equilibrium between the eternal and created time with its lived and cosmological features. Accordingly, the Genesis narrative is overflowing with action-oriented truth, meaning, and possibilities that pertain to a Christian worldview and way of life in the present and for the future.

O Lord God, please give strength in the midst of tiredness, healing in the midst of pain, light in the midst of darkness, and hope in the midst of despair. As natural disasters, financial meltdowns, and horrific tragedies proliferate, may relief efforts actually be enabled and empowered to get to the people who so desperately need them and may the truth and love of the gospel and your mission be made known in all the earth.

What roll are we to play in God's plan to renew and redeem humanity and the world?

The Heavens and the Earth

– St Augustine

"Often a non-Christian knows something about the earth, the heavens, and the other parts of the world, about the motions and orbits of the stars and even their sizes and distances,... and this knowledge he holds with certainty from reason and experience. It is thus offensive and disgraceful for an unbeliever to hear a Christian talk nonsense about such things, claiming that what he is saying is based in Scripture. We should do all that we can to avoid such an embarrassing situation, lest the unbeliever see only ignorance in the Christian and laugh to scorn."

Following the crucified and risen One is both an arduous task and a marvelous joy. Empowered by the Holy Spirit we can limit defeat, while not becoming arrogant in victory. May God grant us strength and wisdom as we seek to love others and share with them the good news of creation, salvation, and new creation.

If there is no distinction between salvation in Christ and the rest of God's works and ways, then theology and spirituality are reduced to salvation. Christians are in danger (promoting salvation exclusively as they tend to do), of losing the important feature of a theological relation and distinction grounded in the character of God. Here's what I mean:

The saving work of Christ finds its rightful place as a dynamic site on the map of Scripture. Yet, there is a dilemma; salvation alone is an inadequate explanation for the origin and destination of Christian spirituality. That is, the scripturally ordered and historical unfolding of salvation reveals to us that salvation comes into a context: God's existence, a created world, death, covenant, a people, a culture, a time—all of which precede the incarnated person and mission of Jesus. God's salvific act dramatically portrayed in and through the sending of Christ, is related and distinct from what God is doing in the world. This means the Christ event finds its first and wider context in the primacy of God's act of creation; a created world affirmed by God and including humans in community with their Creator.

From The Prelude, Book I, 1805
by William Wordsworth

Oh there is blessing in this gentle breeze
That blows from the green fields and from the clouds
And from the sky: it beats against my cheek,
And seems half-conscious of the joy it gives.
O welcome Messenger! O welcome Friend!
A captive greets thee, coming from a house
Of bondage, from yon City's walls set free,
A prison where he hath been long immured.
Now I am free, enfranchis'd and at large,
May fix my habitation where I will.
What dwelling shall receive me? In what Vale
Shall be my harbour? Underneath what grove
Shall I take up my home, and what sweet stream
Shall with its murmur lull me to my rest?
The earth is all before me: with a heart
Joyous, nor scar'd at its own liberty,
I look about, and should the guide I choose
Be nothing better than a wandering cloud,
I cannot miss my way.

The creation stories in Genesis cause our imaginations to soar. Artists, theologians, and scientists find themselves on the same ground here seeking meaning and finding revelation. Wonder, mystery, beauty, and change take us beyond the visible, yet there are boundaries and limits to our imaginative configurations. Creation is the context for all else that take place in God's world and it is crucial to keep it at the forefront of our perspective of life and death.

Like shafts of light piercing into the depths of darkness, God illumines the world in creation and through Christ. Catch the spherical shaping and seminal configurations.

Envisioning God **/** Scripture and creation are
informers which reveal God sufficiently in a related and
distinct manner. It won't do to merely focus on
Scripture and ignore creation,
nor to center on creation and ignore Scripture.
They are integral partners for knowing more
about God, ourselves, and the world;
therefore they have to be in a tensional dialogue.
Thinking about and relating to God,
understanding ourselves,
and living in the world has to be imaginatively done
with both informers playing a role.

Worship **/** I'd like to explore some thoughts on worship. Worship is praising God for what he has done, is doing, and will do. God has a mission, through Creation, Israel, the Messiah, and ourselves to save, renew, and transform people, and the world. This is a call to worship as a response to God's being and actions. So far, so good. There are no doubt several ways to worship—to perform an act of worship.

Can you name some of these ways?
What do you think about worship?

Fowl and Jones in their stimulating book Reading in Communion, 29, put it this way: "Learning to embody Scripture in our lives, both corporately and personally, requires that we develop specific patterns of acting, feeling and thinking well." And this applies to worship. Worship these days, at least in my view, seems to have so little to do with a focus on a close reading of Scripture.

Why is that?

Does worship in many Christian contexts have more to do with making it up as we go along, a subtle yet radical form of idolatry, than it does with reading Scripture; a reading not only for ourselves, but equally against ourselves? Do we, in this context, end up too often endorsing, rather than undermining, self-deception?

Nature is *related to* and distinct from its Creator. In the emerging creation, the Creator is involved in, but not entrapped by the natural world. Idolatry flourishes in this confusion. Yet, God and nature are not one and the same. This truth is crucial for Christian spirituality, for what we worship is not nature, but the Creator.

What does the natural world, if anything, have to do with our views of God?

God, Creation & Spirituality | Notice in the Genesis 1 and 2 stories *(now would be a good time to open your Bible and study these chapters)* that there is no confusion, in contrast to many versions of spirituality today, between the Creator and the created. In Genesis, God is not nature, nor is God confused with nature. Genesis depicts God as involved with nature, but God is never portrayed as entirely related to or distinct from the created world. | This is an important clarification for at least two reasons. **First**, and more generally, it begins to diminish spirituality confusion. It reveals something of who God is, something of who we are, and something of what nature is: God is Creator and not nature, humans are not God or nature, and nature is created not Creator. **Second**, and more specifically, the clarification allows us to contest theologies and spiritualities that speak of God as being entirely one with the created world (related) or having utterly nothing to do with it at all (distinct). | *Sun, moon and stars are not divine, but do you think they mark out something of the character of God and the world?*

From The Prelude, Book III, 1805
by William Wordsworth

As I had done in daily intercourse
With those delicious rivers, solemn heights
And mountains; ranging like fowl in the air,
I was ill tutor'd for captivity,
To quit my pleasure from month to month,
Take up station calmly on the perch
Of sedentary peace. Those lovely forms
Had also left less space within my mind,
Which, wrought upon instinctively, had found
A freshness in those objects of its love,
A winning power, beyond all other power.

A Christian view of spirituality affirms the truth that there is a creational spirituality. The created world is a world that we are to explore, care for, and sustain. Living and true spirituality does not reject the material world, but engages it in service of God. We are to participate in the world and contribute to bringing goodness to all areas of life. As God has not left creation or humans to desolation, decay, or ultimate death, we should not consent to dying forms of spirituality that have no capacity to redeem the created.
—From Living Spirituality: Illuminating the Path.

I like these words of
Samuel Taylor Coleridge
from *Self Knowledge*,
written around 1832.

And heaven-sprung adage of the olden time!

Say, canst thou make thyself?—Learn first that trade—;

Haply thou mayst know what thyself hast made.

What hast thou, Man, thou darest call thine own?

What is there in thee, Man, that can be known?

Dark fluxion, all unfixable by thought,

A phantom dim of past and future wrought,

Vain sister of the worm,—life, death, soul, clod

Ignore thyself, and strive to know thy God!

Paul's rhetoric of equality in 1 Corinthians 7 is astounding. Not only do the bodies of wives belong to their husbands, but the bodies of husbands belong to their wives. Marriage partners are not free to do what they please with their bodies. Spirituality, therefore, is an earthly-bodily phenomenon. Liberty, asceticism and idolatry, are three false emblems of an overly already-focused spirituality that leads us astray. Misunderstandings abound today. Bodies are worshipped (idolatry), devalued (liberty), or seen as having nothing to do with the spiritual, which is entirely cut off from the physical world (asceticism). The body, in Paul's view—both what it is and what it does—is a key part of living spirituality. Redeem the body.

In a logic of superabundance we find there is an excess of givenesss. God, for example, loves and creates in a superabundant manner that cannot be entirely contained in the material world or captured by language. In this light Genesis 1-3 could be viewed as a limit expression text. That is, the text goes to the limit that language and the natural world can bear pushing the ancient Near Eastern boundaries as far as they could go, without being in any way a comprehensive recounting of beginnings. This type of text not merely prevents knowledge from becoming exhaustive, but it dissuades interpreters from attempting totalizing interpretations that would then defy the limit character of the narrative trajectory. Reading and being read by this text will help us clarify our understanding of God, ourselves, and the world, as we seek to know and be known.

God is the great sculptor in time. Catch the vision of this imagery for yourself and live it out as you sculpt a life that is diversely, creatively, and meaningfully lived to the glory of God.

From The Prelude, Book XIII, 1805
by William Wordsworth

This love more intellectual cannot be
Without imagination, which, in truth,
Is but another name for absolute strength
And clearer insight, amplitude of mind,
And reason in her most exalted mood.
This faculty hath been the moving soul
Of our long labour: we have traced the stream
From darkness, and the very place of birth
In its blind cavern, whence is faintly heard
The sound of waters; follo'd it to light
And open day, accomplished its course
Among the ways of Nature, afterwards
Lost sight of it bewilder'd and engulph'd,
Then given it greeting, as it rose once more
With strength, reflecting in its solemn breast
The works of man and face of human life,
And lastly, from its progress have we drawn
The feeling of life endless, the great thought
By which we live, Infinity and God.

In the passing of each year, as we prepare for autumn and begin to experience the sleeping of the earth in winter, let us continue to be ready and awake to God, so that his love and truth might bear fruit in all of us. Pray that his work would blossom and grow in extravagant ways that would surprise us with hope and joy. In looking forward to spring, be thankful for personal spiritual renewal and the promise that God is out to renew the whole world. Will a focus on creation give us a better understanding of God?

Reading Genesis 1-3 as

the theo-drama of creation

opens it up for dynamic re-interpretation, first of all in the Old Testament itself, and then in the New, and then for the many generations preceding ours, and finally for refiguring *(transforming, changing as a result of* ***being read by the text****)* readers lives today and into the future. This mighty theo-drama represents a script that is a legitimate informer about God and nature, which has the capacity to situate readers on the stage and to refigure their lives in the name of the Creator.

How would you interpret the days of creation in Genesis 1?

From The Prelude, Book V, 1805
by William Wordsworth

A gracious Spirit o'er the earth presides,
And o'er the heart of man: invisibly
It comes, directing those to works of love
Who care not, know not, think not what they do:
. . .
Ye dreamers, the,
Forgers of lawless tales! We bless you then,
Imposters, drivellers, dotards, as the ape
Philosophy will call you: then we feel
With what, and how great might ye are in league,
Who make our wish our power, our thought a deed,
An empire, a possession; Ye who Time
And seasons serve; all Faculties; to whom
Earth crouches, th' elements are potter's clay,
Space like a Heaven fill'd up with Northern lights;
Here, nowhere, there, and everywhere at once.

There is a crescent sliver of blue sky piercing through the mist of the billowing grey fog swirling up from the valley lying steeply below.

God, is that you there?

transformation of the mind

At the beginning of the twelfth chapter of Romans, Paul's letter speaks of how in renewing their minds the Romans would be transformed so that they would better know the will of God. That principle from his letter is still true for us today. In seeking after God's redemptive wisdom, we can know him better, and that begins with how we think.

From The Prelude, Book XIII, 1805
by William Wordsworth

A meditation rose in me that night
Upon the lonely mountain when the scene
Had pass'd away, and it appear'd to me
The perfect image of a mighty Mind,
Of one that feeds upon infinity,
That is exalted by an underpresence,
The sense of God, or whatsoe'er is dim
Or vast in its own being ....

A crucial theological question is central to spirituality. Our concern here is not with something that we feel or experience as "beyond" or "transcendent," but with the issue of *who* is speaking and acting, *who* is calling, and *who* is addressing us. Of course, impersonal entities neither speak nor act, and if we have little or no accurate information about the referent of our spirituality, we should have some serious questions. A real and genuine spiritual connection, through the redemptive work of the crucified One, to the personal God who is actually there beyond us, results in release from sin, a changed heart, and a transformed mind—life amidst the divine community.

—From Living Spirituality: Illuminating the Path

What role does
experience play
in your belief
in God?

In the gospel of Mark, parables

reveal and conceal.

Jesus lays great stress on listening to parables so as to know how to hear. Hearing is not enough though, and Jesus' challenge is that true listening will result in true hearing,
which will produce results for the interested and curious.
The extravagant parabolic dimension incites us:
The more we know how to hear
the more we will hear,
and the more we hear
the more we will respond.

Yet, for disinterested, apathetic, and indifferent ears, parables will be like a joke without a punch line.

Nothing happens.

Dialoguing with someone who has serious questions about the nature of the Bible should be considered a privilege.

Encouraging people to put their questions out on the table is essential.

Taking time to work through questions and learn from them will be rewarding.

The Bible does answer many questions, but of course not all.

Awareness of this truth should not lead us to a spirit of silence, but to promoting a spirit of openness that welcomes questions.

At the same time, it is important to recognize that many questions arise in the context of answers, and those answers end up being sufficient for the purpose and goal of knowledge and living life.

From The Prelude, Book X, 1805
by William Wordsworth

This was the time when all things tending fast
To depravation, the Philosophy
That promised to abstract the hopes of man
Out of his feelings, to be fix'd thenceforth
For ever in a purer element
Found ready welcome. Tempting region that
For Zeal to enter and refresh herself,
Where passions had the privilege to work,
And never heard the sound of their own names;
But, speaking more in charity, the dream
Was flattering to the young ingenuous mind
Pleas'd with extremes, and not the least with that
Which makes the human Reason's naked self
The object of its fervour. What delight!
How glorious! In self-knowledge and self-rule,
To look through all the frailties of the world,
And, with resolute mastery shaking off
The accidents of nature, time, and place,
That make up the weak being of the past,
Build social freedom on its only basis,
The freedom of the individual mind,
Which, to the blind restraints of general laws
Superior, magisterially adopts
One guide, the light of circumstances, flash'd
Upon an independent intellect.

People are searching for humanness, but it's hard to find in churches.
In many churches today Christians are not being taught to be human.
There is a failure to inform believers of these insights:
Creation counts;
they will only find themselves in community with God and the other;
Christ is Lord of all of life;
mind and spirit are crucial for being Godly;
they have a missional calling
and that embracing these realities will lead to transformation—being truly human.

This is the only sure way to a proper understanding and explanation of true selfhood. Christians, of all people, ought to be extending a vision of humanness that makes sense, and ultimately it is the biblical world that does this most truthfully.

What does it mean to be human?

From The Prelude, Book XI, 1805
by William Wordsworth

There are in our existence spots of time,
Which with distinct pre-eminence retain
A vivifying virtue, whence, depressed
By false opinion and contentious thought,
Or ought of heavier or more deadly weight,
In trivial occupations, and the round
Of ordinary intercourse, our minds
Are nourished and invisibly repaired.

Christians are facing two dangers:

Becoming as
entirely ambiguous,
or as
exhaustively certain
as anyone else on matters of knowledge.

When it comes to knowledge, we often tend to embrace the perspective of total ambiguity or complete certainty, in exchange for good and sufficient knowledge, which is truly spiritual.

Watching a video of a church service, I was struck by the hype and spin of so much that represents itself as church. The platitudes and lack of content were shocking. **"Amen"** was the lamentable response of the audience. There was plenty of show and performance, centered on one personality cult or another, but it seems to me this type of act is threatening the core of Christianity, which is located in Father, Son, and Spirit, and the revelation and content of love and truth.

Be radical.
Think. Go ahead.
Thinking about the faith won't hurt, and it's part of being a follower of the crucified and risen One in living spirituality. An informed faith, with the book of Scripture, culture, and nature open will help us be more credible representatives of God's mission to the world.

Many forms of

postmodernism
postmodernism
postmodernism
postmodernism
p o s t m o d e r n i s m

postmodernism today are really an expression of modernism. Extremes reign. Some modernists suppose that reason is the light that will explain everything, while some postmodernists argue it explains nothing. Christianity offers us a third way that is not restricted to these types of polarization. There is a place for reason in the Christian faith, but neither reason nor faith is able to give us all the answers to life's mysteries.

Are we left
powerless
to talk about truth in the face of seemingly endless interpretations?

Wisdom emerges in our lives slowly and sometimes painfully. It invites reflection, question, and struggle. It covers everything from advice on how to take care of daily tasks, to the absurdity of them all. Wisdom, without the illumination of the fear—the awe and reverence—of the Lord, loses its way. For true wisdom relates to living spirituality as it deals with facing life in all its ups and downs. God graciously meets us through our lives as we shape the contours of daily routines and choices, so that we might learn to wisely follow the path to life. The fear—the awe and reverence—of the Lord is the beginning of wisdom. This saying targets a two-dimensional reality: Wisdom as internal—focused on the individual, and as external—situated in a variety of social contexts in the world. Life is to be filled with the gift of the wisdom of God, which applies to the whole of human activity as we forge ahead on the journey.

I like these words from William Wordsworth where he keenly expresses the detrimental effects of rationalism:

From The Prelude, Book X, 1805
by William Wordsworth

Thus I fared,
Dragging all passions, notions, shapes of faith,
Like culprits to the bar, suspiciously
Calling the mind to establish in plain day
Her titles and her honours, now believing,
Now disbelieving, endlessly perplex'd
With impulse, motive, light and wrong, the ground
Of moral obligation, what the rule
And what the sanction, till, demanding proof,
And seeing in everything, I lost
All feeling of conviction....

To better understand God and ourselves,
we have to look at and read three scripts:
Scripture,
nature,
and culture.

Always Reforming | Pompous attitudes, unfounded accusations, prideful rhetorical bantering, and defending one's own church tradition do nothing whatsoever to deal with the biblical text in the exegetical manner it so deeply deserves. When controversies and problems arise regarding tradition, there must be a humble and pain-staking wrestling with the text in order to seek to affirm and critique our predecessors and their views. After all, no one will get it totally right, not least ourselves.

Creating hermeneutical space is essential to dialogue and continuing on in the faith. Yet, theological games, prolific argumentation, tendentious jousting simply ignore this reality and are all too often traits that identify Christians. We need to move away from these types of closed-minded short cuts, which do not serve God, nor are they loving to our brothers and sisters—past, present, or future. Hard work in the text and on the text is the long detour for those willing to question the value of traditions that may or may not be biblical. God is with us on the long journey towards enriched biblical truth and living it out into the world.

A lack of reality and excitement about the Christian life can be due to an untransformed mind and impoverished imagination. When our imaginations are not consciously engaged or fall passively dormant, a transformed mind is not happening and our faith will begin to die. God is there, and this is not a mere matter of analysis or feeling. Rather, being in community with God, as unfolding through imagination, should be the end of the pursuit of truth.

Christians all too often become inoculated against the real. Plagued by inauthentic churches peddling illusions and the deception of unreal images that manifest themselves in misplaced expectations and extravagant regimes, which are then given an illegitimate authority and unwarranted priority, Christians fade from the scene of the real world. We have become all too clever at making it up as we go along, propagating reveries and imagining life to be as it is not. There are many attempts, for a variety of reasons, to live in imaginary worlds of our own making, rather than living through a transformed mind and imagination, from the world and to the world as it is: Vive l'imagination.

Wordsworth's words are striking.

From The Prelude, Book VI, 1805
by William Wordsworth

Imagination! lifting up itself
Before the eye and progress of my Song
Like an unfather'd vapour; here that Power,
In all the might of its endowments, came
Athwart me; I was lost in a cloud,
Halted, without a struggle to break through.
And now recovering, to my Soul I say
I recognize thy glory; in such strength
Of usurpation, in such visitings
Of awful promise, when the light of sense
Goes out in flashes that have shewn to us
The invisible world, doth Greatness make abode,
There harbours whether we be young or old.

Take some time to recognize and be thankful
for the importance and relevance of
imagination
when it comes to belief in God.

Might we be living *in times where what we have known as church and culture are falling apart and beginning to disintegrate? And if so, where are we going to turn to find renewal and hope? If Western culture and church are to be revived, fervent prayer and the power of the Spirit will be essential. Further, I believe that one of the crucial elements of recovery will have to be a deep commitment to the reading, study, and appropriation of Scripture. Living the practices embedded in the biblical text is central to Christian existence and having an impact on church and culture for the sake of Christ.*

When it comes *to the Christian faith, don't be afraid to improvise. That does not mean to make it up as we go along, but to join in with the symphony of Scripture and to find your place in interpreting and becoming part of the composition.*

**What role, if any,
does imagination play in reading Scripture?**

Often existential anxiety drives the fears of losing self, meaning, and truth.
Yet, the unwillingness to turn away from being one's own authority increases.
Generally, a hardness of heart and a lack of openness characterize much of the Western mindset as it becomes fixated on itself and gives up on the possibility of finding adequate responses to its fears.
By contrast to that which drives our age, we desperately need to return
to the God who is love,
to truth that is sufficiently livable,
to redemption in Christ, and
to the power of the Spirit
—all of which can contribute to breaking the cycle of fear and to finding ourselves.

Do you think there's a place for the self in Christian spirituality?

There are often strong poles drawn between ***teaching about*** *God and having a luminous* ***experience of*** *God. Why? For some people these appear to be our "either/or" options. Teaching and knowledge are perceived as negative and they may well be misused, while a holy embracing of luminous experience becomes the pinnacle of goodness, and some experiences may well be like that. In this scenario, we now have the false option of having to choose experience of God over knowledge of God. Most would choose the experience. Yet, all teaching is not necessarily bad and any luminous experience not necessarily good. Critical insight and assessment are essential. "Both/and" should be pursued.*

From The Prelude, Book II, 1805
by William Wordsworth

Thus did my days pass on,
and now at length
From Nature and her overflowing soul
I had receiv'd so much
that all my thoughts
Were steep'd in feeling; I was only then
Contented when with bliss ineffable
I felt the sentiment of Being spread
O'er all that moves,
and all that seemeth still,
O'er all, that, lost beyond
the reach of thought
And human knowledge, to the human eye
Invisible, yet liveth to the heart

Our cultures frequently banalize or ignore God and truth. As the pressures of extreme forms of postmodernisms develop and new expressions of pantheism and pragmatism rise and gain a foothold in our cultures, we want to be able to think clearly and to love boldly. Insight and direction, combined with compassion and grace, are crucial for knowing how to navigate through the high degree of confusion in today's world and for seeking to follow in the footsteps of the crucified and risen One.

Thinking
seriously
about
important
matters is
a Christian
responsibility.
To attempt to
ignore people
and what's going
on in the world
is not a virtue,
but a defect.
To assume that
a Christian
should have
an empty mind
is not spiritual,
but unspiritual.
To the contrary,
engaging ideas
and people—
for the sake of
Christ—is being a
spiritual witness
to what is true.

From The Prelude, Book XII, 1805
by William Wordsworth

Dearest Friend,
Forgive me if I say that I, who long
Had harbour'd reverentially a thought
That Poets, even as Prophets, each with each
Connected in a mighty scheme of truth,
Have each for his peculiar dower, a sense
By which he is enabled to perceive
Something unseen before; forgive me, Friend,
If I, the meanest of the Band, had hope
That unto me had also been vouchsafed
An influx, that in some sort I possess'd
A privilege, and that a work of mine,
Proceeding from the depth of untaught things,
Enduring and creative, might become
A power like one of Nature's.

The consumer church has adopted a new trinity of culture, experience, and feeling as its primary authority. This is a cadence we don't want to follow. Tangled webs of interconnection with these three run so deep that Christians find themselves trapped in and saturated by that which is not of God. Sapped of resistance to the banal and overwrought by appearances, Divine meaning begins to dissipate, and Christian truth and faith become irrelevant to the church and the watching world. It's time for this to change and take a new direction. A return to Scripture and the art of reading it will open up possibilities for breaking away from the former empty indulgences and beginning anew.

Christian culture is all too often rooted in the dominating sub-text of false guilt, fear and shame. There's no room in this space for the sacred text, which is squeezed out by the imposition of powerful and manipulating forces that are far from the gospel. Christians, in these contexts, are drastically deprived from being shaped and informed by the biblical text. Impoverishment is the lamentable result. Creating time and space for skillful Bible reading and study is essential for engaging, challenging, and then going beyond the sub-text. Such efforts will bring to light fresh insights and new possibilities of redemption, grace and freedom.

Idolatry and Feelings

Idolatry often takes place in the feelings world and is not necessarily connected to an external, physical, material reality. The present way we feel may be our ultimate authority and therefore result in idolatry. From a Christian perspective, any felt lack or euphoria inside is not the whole of a life story.

We all too easily deceive ourselves.

Our feelings may or may not be telling us the truth. Once we include the may not in this configuration the world explodes, as we find we can no longer assume that what we feel is unconditionally and necessarily true. We feel it, and there is no doubt about that, but just because we feel something is not a definitive reason to believe that what is felt is true. What takes place inside us and what reigns in our lives has to be questioned:

What is true?

the real narrative

Each of us has a story.
This story, or narrative, is comprised of our memories, beliefs, experiences, and is seen through the lens of a worldview. Our individual perspective is unique, and yet we share commonalities with those in our families, communities, and cultures. As we attempt to discern truth, we need to humbly recognize that we do not simply impose our view on the world; reality speaks back to us and informs us, as well. When we enter into a dialogue with reality, this dialogue can begin to help us form a more consistent and accurate narrative. There are several informers we need to pay attention to and Scripture is one of the main one's for Christians. We move into dangerous territory, however, (i.e. the Bible becoming a god that we worship) if we decide that Scripture is the only way of understanding life in the world. Recognizing the significance of the grand story that Scripture portrays will enable us to ascertain our role in its narrative; keeping in mind that we are joining in the story that began thousands, if not millions, of years ago. Yet, as our own stories unfold, let's remember there are many dialogical threads to engage with including reality, our cultures, the world, and Scripture.

In the Beginning **|** *The founding narrative in Genesis, this story of beginnings, sets out a theological, historical, and literary re-description of the world, which stands in polemical contrast to other ancient Near Eastern portrayals of creation, as well as contemporary forms of naturalism. This organization of theological actions, temporal relations, and a phenomenological description of the world comes about through the construction of a plot with the collective expression of past, present, and future. Wisdom flows from the past about living as God would like and precedes Genesis, while salvation in the future streams out and extends beyond it, yet both dimensions of time are intercalated within the writing of the narrative, as it presently unfolds God's story.*

As readers of the scriptural story today, we are foreigners to the text and its ancient Near Eastern and Greco-Roman context, yet we are not excluded from its time, narration, drama, and spherical refraction. The possibility remains for us to be grafted into the revelatory story of God's creation and redemptive outpouring of love in Christ, which offers us a place on the stage of the cosmic drama of life. Renewing people and the earth is part of God's majestic story.

Fortunately, we're invited to participate.

Two Stories

There are two stories in conflict throughout the Christian journey.

The first is	The second is
the story	the story
of the	of the
truth,	lie,
creation,	uncreation,
promise,	deception,
redemption	fear, and
and hope,	hopelessness,
which	which
results in	brings
life.	death.

These two stories battle for a primary authority, control, and for ultimate direction. Recounting itself over and over, the second story just doesn't disappear, and may grip us deeply. Things in this world sometimes seem pointless and without meaning. A recurring thought is—is it worth it? Yet, the first story is still more potent and dominant, because it is true. The world is full of meaning—even a surplus of meaning. It is worth it.

Have you read a good story recently? What's so compelling about good stories?

The Bible is not God.

In many circles of Christianity, I fear, there is a growing bibliolatry that assumes that having and reading the Bible is enough. This ignores the truth that the Bible itself points us past itself to an encounter with the living God, who invites us into community with him.

Text and encounter
are essential to a vibrant and living spirituality.

Reflect on the trans-historicity,
that is the durability,
of the narrative of Scripture. What a marvel. Revealed in a historical context, which remains important, the story nevertheless goes far beyond its context and reaches out and touches lives throughout time and space history.

Scripture, God's story, is founded on temporality, but flourishes on excess, because God is a God of excess; we'll never come to the end of who he is.

Biblical narrative is the most astounding drama engaging God and humanity. This drama goes far beyond a dispassionate or detached recounting or a merely experiential endeavor. God's story is closer to the way things really are, than any notion of story told from the point of clinical neutral observation or heightened spiritual experience. We find ourselves as Christians on the global and local stage of the working out of the drama by actualizing it in our own lives.

Exodus remains a central and remarkable phase in the self-revelation of God and the life of God's people. Living spirituality is never far from the double focus of this founding event: Release and justice. Live in memory of the Exodus, and apply its outcome to oneself and all of life.

*Informed by the script of Scripture
and a new reality brought by Christ,*

we're called to live imaginatively engaged lives. Rather than having media and contemporary culture imagine for us what life is to be like, let's imagine being an other and walking in their shoes, so that we might serve them better. Acting with compassion, interest, and love should be trademarks that identify Christians, as we imaginatively seek to follow in the footsteps of Christ. Serving God and others requires a living and an empowered imagination.

It's all too easy, and in spite of best intentions, to control and dominate Scripture to the degree that it loses its voice for us. In reading Scripture, let's be open to transformation and new ways of seeing. Monologues are demanding and change nothing. Dialogue takes risks and requires courage. Be risky and courageous. Hear the text well, perform it in a fitting manner, and live.

Demonstrating a Divine Drama | Surfacing into the Divine drama from under the weight of careless formulations and clinical apologetics should produce improvised stage performances that shock a dreadfully impoverished audience into action for the sake of Christ. There may be those who take offence at such high level commitment. So be it. ***Woe*** to the disinterested and self-righteous. God is not honored by superficiality and trite jargon that has no impact on a watching world. Better performances of the script—living the truth in word and deed, will give a greater credibility to our testimony for the sake of Christ.

Scripture is a script to be enacted,
not merely some foundation for knowledge or a deposit of ancient words.
God is the great dramaturge who sets out the drama
of redemption as a communicative action.
This is not a secret buried in the recesses of tombs,
but a testimony to light and life.
We are not left out of the play,
but in Christ invited
to be part of
the action,
cultivating wisdom through Word and Spirit so that we might act in faithful and fitting ways.

The target or goal of the words of Scripture is to reveal God. The words don't refer to themselves, but to God and to what God has done, is doing, and will do to renew and redeem us and the world. They recount, report, jive, jump, skid, symbolize, and want us to have an ever deepening experience of the reality of being in community with Father, Son, Spirit and each other.

Roaming | Recently on a hike through the Swiss Alps nearby our chalet, I was struck again not only by the beauty, but also by the problematic of perception. Winding my way up the mountain side I kept reflecting on how at different points in the journey perceptions change, yet the goal to get to the top of the mountain remains the same. Being in community with God, I believe, has some inviting similarities. When we are in one place, life appears to be a certain way, but then a different vista opens up as we go on and gain elevation, we see more than we did previously. In community with God and the journey towards our destiny of being transformed into the image of Christ, there will be some steeper bits that require effort and commitment leading to in-Spirited new perceptions, while at other times what we perceive will be like walking in the same place for a time.

Free From Death | The powerful and enticing character of death sometimes sweeps over us like pelting sheets of freezing rain. In the fast paced narrative of destruction, I find myself on the edge of the garden, relentlessly attempting to re-enter, but to no avail. The direction is forward to life, and God is there. Thankfully, I'm not lost in the circle of the same that brings imagination and creativity to the graveyard of folly. I am free.

A traumatic encounter with the living God leaves us shaken with awe and wonder. Come, oh Lord, and awaken us from our slumber. Create in us clean hearts, engraved with love and a peace that passes all understanding.

What is an experience of God and is it different than other experiences?

Contextual Theology | Speaking of God in the world brings forth many voices. Stories are told from a variety of cultural contexts and it is inevitable that we have to take these into consideration when reading Scripture. Telling stories is an essential part of life and the understanding of self-identity. In many ways our stories validate our lived experience. | Here's the issue I'd like you to consider: Many Christians today are moving in the direction of embracing lived experience as the basis for their theology. Taking seriously the valid role of lived experience as a source for theology, some now contend it has become its only norm. Theology is nothing more than an expression of lived Christian experience. Given the fact that we live in a multi-cultural world and have different experiences of God, these experiences are said to be what defines us. I'm African, Asian, Canadian, American, European, and so on. One of the most prominent questions we face is to what degree our experience should shape and form our view of ourselves and God. | *How do you see it? What role should experience have in our theological formulations?*

Words, words, and more than words.

Being a follower of the crucified and risen One is not a word rehearsal, but a performance. Performing is deeply connected to knowing the script (Scripture) and to the direction (Spirit) of the cast. If we are to produce a stellar and faithful recounting of the story line, it is time to see ourselves in radically fresh ways. We are part of the theodrama – the troupe of performers who have a role in God's mission to the world.

Mark's gospel is full of role reversals.

Those who think they see and hear are **blind and deaf**,
and those who are blind and deaf, **see and hear**.

A in-spirited and storied life of following Jesus is not about possessing people and things but about dispossession; being willing to let go, take risks, to be courageous, and to not to fear. To be great, you have to be least; the first will be last, and the last first. Those who want to save their lives will have to lose them for the sake of Jesus and the gospel. And in perhaps one of the most striking reversals of all in Mark's narrative it is the demons and unclean spirits who know who Jesus is, while the disciples don't—go figure.

Reading the Parables | Jesus' parables aim to subvert and shatter, while reconstructing in the wake of the debris. What happens in these powerful stories is bursting with meaning that dangerously engages the imagination. The attacking and overturning character of parables is not to be missed. Parables also disorient, shock, and surprise, bringing about reversal and re-orientation in the disclosing of a new understanding concerning the person of Jesus, the world, the Kingdom of God, and the hearer.

There is nothing more spiritual, no other way of having the fullness of life, than following the crucified and risen One, which is both a joy and a task.

The long waited arriving of the Kingdom of God in Jesus' day and its dynamic and ongoing presence in our own should be understood as something radical, which overturns and shatters the status quo. God was and is doing something new in Christ, including extending an invitation to those considered outsiders, beyond the realm of God's healing and forgiveness. While welcoming outsiders, the mission and message of the Kingdom of God critiques the religious elite, who tend to see themselves as insiders and keepers— at all costs—of the status quo.

Philippians is a wonderful letter.
Have a read. It's only four chapters.
Whatever our present circumstances,
we are to see our lives in a larger context.
Present circumstances are important, but they shouldn't control us because our lives are directed to a greater destiny—to image Christ. As humans, we tend to be so integrated in the present, so overwhelmed by it, that we see the present as all that matters. But the epistle to the Philippians encourages us to recognize that present circumstances are not our final reality—whether joy or suffering. We should be careful not to be lured too deeply into either good or bad present circumstances as if they are all that count for the Christian life.

In our culture today, the issue of **economics** *is front page news. Never before has there been such a proliferation of information on world markets. The markets and all that is connected to them are becoming god-like and our fate and destiny are supposedly tied to their very survival. But in watching this development carefully, we are seeing more global unification in the attempt to salvage life as we once knew it. Too late. Everything will have to change. The closer we get to an international group of the masters of the economy, the greater danger there is of control and manipulation. And, of course, this is all in the name of security and protection. Keep a watchful eye open for what unfolds next in these unprecedented times.*

A World of Paper Currency | As trillions of dollars, euro, pounds, yen, and so forth disappear into the deep dark hole of government spending, I wonder if the world of recovery is not more of an illusion, than a reality. There are so many subterfuges, dishonesties, and covert activities, we may be coerced into believing that this is just the way that it is, and we have no choice but to get used to it. We are increasingly living in a world of image without referent, sign without signifier, and language without meaning. Economics and politics reign in today's world as never before in history, and when that happens, recovery in any true sense will prove to be unachievable.

The plight of much of the Western church ***is that it has been highly influenced by its culture's politics, economics, and society. Instead of always following current trends, Christians need to take the lead and find biblical, creative, and spiritual ways to bring the truth and love of the gospel into the world. Redeeming our political, economic, and social relations is a crucial—even primordial—task that requires our serious attention and our devoted time and energy. As far as I see it, this redemption can begin on a local scale and grow from there. Change is possible – the status quo is death – we can make an effort to bring our communities and churches life as we seek to apply biblical truths and a renewed worldview.***

In the theater of life let's aim for a focus on mission, living spirituality, truth, honesty, community with God and each other, concern for the poor, the environment, culture, the arts, and the authenticity of redemption. A fitting performance counts, and we all have an important role to play.

Metaphor, Story, and Symbol | Rather than secondary, ornamental, or aesthetic renderings of what is real, metaphor, symbol and story may be first order forms of discourse that need to be taken seriously as we seek to understand God, ourselves, and the world. Poetry, for example, may be a fuller expression of truth than mathematical formulations, and narrative imagination may prove a reliable guide to the real over the unreal.

God is not out to turn us into zeroes or zombies. He addresses and calls us through grace to respond to his offer of salvation and to being in community with him. This means we have to show up, to be accounted for, to be responsible, and to use what we have, in order to appreciate and enjoy the freedom that God gives.

From Aids to Reflection, Aphorism XXV, 1825, by Samuel Taylor Coleridge

He who begins by loving Christianity better than Truth, will proceed by loving his own sect or Church better than Christianity, and end in loving himself better than all.

The times are mystifying. Everyone is searching for a spiritual life. One person goes this way, another that. So many trends and options are available today. In the midst of the driving enthusiasm and obsessive quest for a spiritual life, spirituality has come to mean everything, yet nothing. Christians have to help lead the way out of the maze by embracing and living the truths of the faith. We should seek to embody and hope to demonstrate the existence of God, the redemption of Christ, and the power of the Spirit.

Improvising is not about doing something entirely new. Think of it this way: To improvise is to join in, to recognize that we are part of a work in progress; something that precedes us. Faithful improvisation is listening to and speaking for others. To participate in God's story in following the crucified and risen One is to respond to an invitation to improvise.

Christian truth is far from maintaining the status quo. It challenges the arrogant powers and despotic tyrants that seek to possess and control the world. Christ came to defeat sin, to overthrow evil, to bring life, to open possibilities, to affirm change, and to inaugurate transformation.

What's happening to our world?

We find ourselves in unprecedented times.

We've never been here before.

Yes, the world's previously been a mess,

but the scale of our plight has now

dramatically increased:

Financial markets are crumbling and in turmoil,

natural catastrophes are creating havoc and destruction,

governments are run by incompetent

and sometimes corrupt elected officials.

In addition, political sovereignty is awfully close

to being a consumer product,

and much of the Western church

is not only ineffective and woefully impoverished,

but it is losing credibility

and its very existence is under serious threat.

OUR CULTURAL NARRATIVE OF CONSUMERISM AND SELF-CENTEREDNESS HOLDS OUT GREAT TEMPTATIONS TO ALLOW OURSELVES TO BE CONSUMED. IT'S OFTEN SO MUCH EASIER TO GO WITH THE FLOW THAT LEADS TO DEATH, THAN IT IS TO BE AGENTS OF LIFE. LET'S REMEMBER TO BE PARTAKERS IN AND MESSENGERS OF LOVE, REDEMPTION, AND FORGIVENESS AS WE LIVE OUT THE CHRISTIAN STORY IN THE FULLEST AND MOST MEANINGFUL WAY POSSIBLE.

Self 1

A decentered self is crucial for self-understanding and the critique of a false self. That is, self- centeredness is a problem and decentering is therefore appropriate if we are to make our way towards being true selves. A true self is a self that is not centered on itself, but on Christ. God wants us to be true selves. Therefore, stopping at decentering; never surpassing the appropriate will be insufficient. We are called to move further and to embrace a recentering, which culminates in community with God, through Christ.

Self 2

Since we have no direct access to self, we can come nowhere near being in full possession of ourselves. This means we are to be open to intervention, mediation, and information. Being a self shaped by the biblical text and the natural world provides us with sufficient resources for making a good start. Self-understanding is notably an important part of God understanding although neither, in this life, will reach completion. Yet, already now it is important to be a new self and to imagine being a new self in Christ as portrayed in the New Testament's image of what might it be to be called a true self.

Self 3

Since we live in a world of radical relation and distinction, being a self shaped by God, the biblical text, the natural world, and the other illuminates the path towards explanatory power and new understanding. Many today aim at self mastery through reason, consciousness, or seeing. They attempt to be autonomous or self-contained selves who recount their own stories as omniscient narrators. Nothing could be further from the truth or further from who we are as human beings.

Self 4

We are summoned, yet irreplaceable selves (there is not another us) called out of the illusion of being 'I' by the Other and others. Any notion of being true selves is irreducible to the "what and why" of identity. The key question that cannot be bypassed: Who is responding, speaking, and acting? Understanding our story is crucial. Breakdowns in who is recounting create discontinuity and an inability to connect and move through the story with a coherent reading. The fragile character of temporal experience is deeply integrated into who we have been, presently are, and eventually will be.

What role, if any, does self-deception still play in the Christian life?

The drama of redemption is not merely "Jesus saves me," but it includes God's mission to the natural,
cultural,
social,
economic,
racial and
political dimensions—the whole stage of reality. God is out to redeem and renew the world. This theodrama begins at

creation,

follows through to

redemption,

and culminates in

renewal.

Let's find our parts on the stage
and in humility and grace
act them out skillfully
with flair and passion.

Real and Unreal | The perplexing enigma of real and unreal has brought our culture to a place in time where some thinkers and writers, combined with the intellectual climate in many universities today, embrace the perspective that we now find ourselves in a post-modern, post-Christian, post-history, post-real, post-human world. In this story, images are always images of images, of images, of images. It's image, which translates into unreal, all the way down. *What is real? How can Christians stand for the real in an age of the unreal?*

Our reading strategies for Scripture, self, other, and the world should have a similarity. That is, not too objective, nor too subjective. These phenomena are not to be mere objects of analysis and study or simply personal subjects of possession and interest, but understood as related and distinct in tension. Falling into compartmentalized or collapsed approaches will lead to a short circuiting of making necessary tensional connections that will enhance and deepen our spirituality. These connections will help us to recognize that there are new possibilities and fresh discoveries that pave the way for drawing closer to God, his truth, and love, and then living it out into the world.

Our imaginations play a crucial role in knowing God, ourselves, others, and the world. How we picture these communities, through our hearts and minds as revealed in Scripture and nature will have a tremendous impact on how we live as God's children. Engaging, transforming, redeeming, and sanctifying imaginations are part of God's aim to renew the world and bring us more fully into his awesome and loving presence.

Cycles and patterns of defeat can all too often be prominent in the life of a Christian. Transformation and renewal will not take place by an attempt to simply modify these powerful self identity symptoms, as they usually are a result or manifestation of something much deeper. That is, for sustainable change to arise it is essential to explore the core of who we are. God wants to get to this core; to our hearts, and the picture we have of him as God and ourselves as his children. Growing freedom from perpetual defeat comes about through Christ being at the center of our lives, which radically gives us a new picture and releases us to choose and live life.

Reflection

The fragility of life
breaks through and haunts us at various times.
We're never ready to face our worst fears,
though there is not much that we can do to prepare for them.
Life is something like that.
Heartbreak traces itself upon our desires
and etches its way onto our flesh and spirit.
Yet, redemption is our weapon
and hope is our shield
against the onslaught of human brokenness,
and its consequences for those who live in the world.

the Exodus
church

Church Epitaph

Long ago love had been lost,
Won over so easily
By the ever changing winds of fortune
Swept away by spending more than any cost

Rocky shores prevented ships from docking
To bring cherished cargo,
New resources to those starving in safe
White buildings with blinking crosses

Navigating sovereign thickets,
Falling till it didn't matter anymore
Waiting on streets of hope
Truth blocked and sealed the doors and windows

Spellbound hiding in warping blindness
Blood dripped from dead dogs eyes,
Follow me, I'll lead you heavenward
What ever your dreams conceive in clean
White buildings with blinking crosses

Sterile laws beckon
To those seeking cleansing here,
Baptized in shame and guilt pervading
Loosen the dam and let freedom flow
Streaming from a cross neglected,
Buried under hearts of stone

Soliciting alms while
Prostitutes, vagrants, strangers assailing,
A losing trick to keep from finding escape
Suffocating inside the walls of fated
White buildings with blinking crosses

Grace untold, the secret kept
To those forgetting where it
Blossoms from created
Earthen hollowed trees and
Spacious fields of vine and branch

Pierced illusions never fading promoted,
Oh deathly sacramental longings betrayed
On the register of time exploding
White buildings with blinking crosses

Like a death wish
But to the funeral no one came for only
To cease from experiencing a moment's charade
Was too much to ask of those slain in wonder, praise,
and fame

The Exodus Church—Part 1 | What I'm calling the Exodus Church may be another way of talking about the need for a new Church. Here's why I refer to it as an Exodus Church: This church is a body of people that belong to Christ, which is fleeing from mainline and fundamentalist churches. It is emerging out of the arid and stifling atmosphere of Egypt and heading towards the living water of the Promised Land, but it needs the map of Scripture, creation, and the directedness of the Spirit to find the way. Living in "Egypt" enslaves God's people, while following the crucified and risen One brings release and eventual entry into the Promised Land. But the path to the Promised Land is arduous and we need God and each other. There are several characteristics that begin to identify this Exodus church and its concerns. Here are six.

1) Truthful - missional
2) Redemptive - communal
3) Finding - searching
4) Creational - environmental
5) In-Spirited - spiritual
6) Loved - loving

What are several characteristics that you think should identify

CHURCH?

The Exodus Church—Part 2 | Prominent notions of Exodus form

of pain,

of renewal,

of disappointment,

a nucleus around the themes

of hope and

of betrayal,

of lament,

redemption.

Exodus continues. The journey of wilderness wandering, in the company of God, will lead toward new beginnings, and one fine day we will all arrive in the Promised Land. In the meantime, we are in this time in-between times ....

A Plea from those who are Battle Torn and Worn, longing for New Beginnings:

Conflicts are brewing at an alarming pace between Christians who are emerging and those who are not. Fine – let's discuss what we have in common and where we disagree. But please, for the sake of Christ Jesus, let's do this with grace, love, humility, and a flair for holiness, as we live before the watching world. There has been too much—and it must be said with tears—spiteful innuendo, anger, disrespect, and injustice in the past. Let's not repeat that in the present. These battles get ugly and there is no winner. The numbers of wounded merely increase and the love of Christ pales into obscurity. We are torn and worn by the wars. Release us, oh Lord, and give us a new beginning.

Give voice to those who long to be free—let us speak of some important matters.

We believe *it is essential to love God, each other, and all people.*

We believe *it is crucial to turn our hearts and minds to God and in so doing, to worship, to encounter God, not just to talk or read about God.*

We believe *we are actors in the great drama of God's global mission of redemption and the renewal of all things, centered in and upon the crucified and risen One.*

We believe *Scripture and Spirit reveal God, refresh our memories, empower our imaginations, and direct our lives into a deepening community with God and each other.*

We believe *that Jesus is Lord, and that churches or Empires are not.*

We believe *the drastic slippage into church activities, committees, buildings and bureaucratic mumbo-jumbo being central, results in deep spiritual impoverishment. Tear down the walls – let the people go – let us go. Following in the footsteps of Christ will bring freedom for the oppressed and disenfranchised.*

We believe *the arts, and cultural participation and analysis are vital.*

We believe *in church as community, as a Scripture reading and living community.*

We believe *in hospitality and a compassionate welcoming of strangers.*

We believe *that the Christian life is an expression of living spirituality. Living spirituality is both verb and adjective. It is to be lived, and it is living. Living because God is a living God and lived because we are spiritual people.*

The Exodus Church—Part 3 | We see myriads of churches have gone the way of the institution. "Christian" becomes institutional, or a lukewarm religious definition too often characterized by an indifferent "pop-spirituality" that seems far from engaging with people and their real issues and problems. Churches can be—and it must be said with tears—primarily interested in propagating their programs, building their buildings, even manipulating some of their own, in order to achieve social status and accomplish their goals and purposes. Even as Christians today desperately strive for the authentic, they have never before been so captured by that which is inauthentic. Thwarted by "shopping" and "shuffle" spirituality, cultural materialism, and the syrupy sweetness of comfortable idealism, living spirituality becomes a mirage and Christian credibility seriously wanes.

We may become extremely suspicious as to whether there is even a link between the words Christian and spirituality – alas, so much talk and so little action. The large gap between words and actions strikes us as problematic. In engaging with those who call themselves Christians, we observe hollow and superficial ideologies and practical lives that fail to reflect the face of Christ. A lamentable lack of the reality of love, of authenticity, and the "real" become reasons for avoiding all things and people labeled Christian.

Life's important questions go unanswered, and the reality of holistic, interactive, and interpretive living spirituality is acutely absent. Cold, mechanical, forced religiosity or warm, fuzzy superficiality will rightly bring forth suspicion, apathy, and rejection by those who have valid concerns about what is authentic and true.

We see the land is still arid here Lord and our hearts are parched. *We can't stay in the desert for we shall die. Thankfully, God is liberating people who thirst for more. Leaving the graveyards and tombstones behind, we are longing for the kingdom of God and the renewal of all things. We readily confess our sin and cry out for redemption. We are on our way to new beginnings.* Please, Lord, lead us forward. *Exodus.*

We are crying as the Exodus Church, and yet part of the people of God. We are seeking to move closer to our destiny of being transformed into the image of Christ, leaving behind the wounds of promising words that give the pretense of care and concern, but translate into intolerable levels of neglect and inconsistent waffling.

We desperately cling to being in community with God and others, and long to participate in and live for God's mission to the world through Jesus and the power of the Spirit.

Something's going on here. It's already taking place. Theodrama. The Exodus journey has begun. New beginnings result in following in the footsteps of Christ. The power of redemption and the personal agency of the Spirit open the way for this to begin to take place; we're grateful.

Help us, oh God, to live the truth in
refreshing and life-giving ways.
We hope that our wilderness wanderings
will contribute to greatly diminishing
spiritual impoverishment and to
dramatically increasing love
for you, each other, and the world.

The Exodus Church—Part 4 | Hopefully, we will make a contribution towards cultivating mission and renewal in our land as we awaken to the stark reality of the power of stagnation and death surrounding us on many fronts.

Mass Exodus is taking place. Lamentably, there are churches that have fallen into spiritual adultery; the intercourse of legalism, manipulation, self-service, consumerism, and arrogance controls their essence and message. Clearly, not all churches should be viewed in this manner; however—and it must be said with weeping—there are far too many who fit into this woeful description. Many people in spiritually adulterous churches have had enough and are coming out. A renewed searching for truth, spiritual survival, and direction are underway.

As for us, we confess our own sin and long for release. We are being liberated out of the cycle of slavery in Egypt, but the wounds of enslavement run deep, and we are limping through the wilderness with God carrying us along as necessary. We're grateful to be here. Bring us healing, dear God.

In our wilderness wanderings, we experience freedom; we are learning to find our way ahead as we begin to break loose from the chains that enslaved us. Mind, heart, spirit, all cry for restoration. We are better now in the wilderness—at least we're free—but we need direction for the journey in order to reach our destination. We face the challenges of spiritual impoverishment and attractions to the dying. To be sure, we're exposed to many paths.

Lord we ask that you will lead us together into life – to forming and being real communities of truth and life. Feed us, oh God, with the manna of your word and through the power of the Spirit, so that as we seek to follow in the footsteps of the crucified and risen One, we may be transformed and radiate your missional presence in the world.

Facing the plight of indifference in church and culture, we promise to make an effort to embody the biblical mandate of living a greater consistency between our words and actions. This is crucial and hugely relevant. Words, words and more words go nowhere. It is our words and actions together that count. Let's seek to be places of refuge—shelters in the wilderness so that we find the way together in unity. Following Christ into the power of redemption and the personal agency of the Spirit unlock the door for this to begin to take place. That is, who we are, what we say, and what we do are all relevant to the mission of Christ and being the Exodus Church. Authenticity is essential. Being truthful, real, hopeful, vulnerable, and even sacrificial is now up to us. We long to be every-day people living in the real world – wilderness though it may be. To both stand for the truth and live for the truth in love in the most subversive of ways and deeds is a high calling. Far too often we fail to express love to those both inside and outside of the Christian community – release us from this, oh Lord, and create in us a new heart. Through renewal and transformation we will be able to show Christ's love to each other, fellow sojourners, and all people. The beauty of active Christian love is compelling, and it helps others to acknowledge that God is with us. Love is one of the chief characteristics of mission and without it we shall surely fail.

We look to the Spirit and the reality
of being wilderness wanderers to translate the
crucified and risen One's words of love, hope,
compassion, honesty, and integrity into actions.
This looking and translating is a key
characteristic of living spirituality.
Of course, this is never perfect, and at
times it will break down. Still, as we live in the
wilderness, there is to be a continual attempt
to demonstrate a transformed life for the sake
of—and to the
glory of—God.
We see more
clearly now
that in our
wilderness
wanderings
a biblical
spirituality
desperately
needs to be
taught and lived
in deep, loving,
cutting-edge
ways within the
wilderness, if
we are going to begin to
reverse impoverishment and
the allure of the dying, as we
take God's mission to
the world. May God
bless our efforts
for Jesus' sake.

The Exodus Church—Part 5 | Prominent trends in Western culture tend to attempt to give everyone a spiritual and cultural lobotomy – the trite and superficial, silly and absurd, brain dead and uncreative often identify Westerners in general, and Christians in particular. Our inevitable plight is that we're always following close behind.

We are experiencing the deep psychosis of cultural despotism that is thoroughly soaked into our Christian flesh and blood, leaving us with empty imaginations. Our bones are disintegrating before our eyes, our bowels are exploding, and there is no strength left in our guts. Too much "fast food" spirituality. Are we stupid or what?

Instead of subverting, challenging, and rebelling, instead of leading our culture into redemptive ways, into release from captivity, Christians tamely and politely do what everyone else is doing— participate in the lobotomy. Hail bureaucracy, church, and the free market, which make for the good life. What a joke. Following the crucified and risen One and not thoughtless, frivolous Western culture is our Exodus.

We're enchanted by nothing and starving from an overdose of sweetness, indifference, and doctrinalitis that blinds us to the task at hand. Our missional strategy, in the best sense of that overused metaphor, and our love for the other, are lying dead in Western streets and churches. Tombstones wave flags to those passing by, directing them in the way to the graveyard. Surrounded, invaded, and captured by this spiritual and cultural perspective, our desperate need for Exodus is intensifying by the moment.

God, bring us out and into the land of the living. Provoke a dramatic shift in our part in your mission to the world so that we might share in your passion for people, for truth, and for saving us sinners. We must all count ourselves lost aside from your mercy and grace, which you extraordinarily seek to bestow upon us. Free us from the cultural and spiritual lobotomizing taking place in our churches and renew and re-shape us in Kingdom fitting ways that confront and expose the allure of Empire glorification.

Where are the churches that promote cutting-edge thinking and living before the watching world? They're few and far between. **What is piercing our churched hearts?** *God's superabundance? Living spirituality? Mission? Loving others? Not likely.*

Too often it seems that what concerns us most is the Empire idol of socio-economic status and prosperity; which is equivalent to lobotomy. Such a mesmerizing charade works like a scalpel cutting off vital pieces of our brains and hearts, and will lead us nowhere. Let's get real and start thinking again. Once we get our brains and hearts back, we can join the conversation, and then generate action, powered by the Spirit in alignment with God's truth and mission. Credibility and authenticity are found in following the crucified and risen One, which creates and culminates in Exodus.

Forging communities drenched in the theodrama of Father, Son, and Holy Spirit, where we all have a part on the grand stage of Exodus (social, racial, political, economic, cultural, redemptive) will enhance missional love and acceptance, illuminating teaching, trenchant wisdom, and hope for the present and future.

What are some of the

of attending church?

What are we to make of

in the church today?

The Exodus Church—Part 6 | There is an acute and desperate need for creating genuine, savvy, and missional Christian communities. The state of so many churches today is lamentable. Churches exist in abundance, but many thinking people today are fleeing them, or sitting on the sidelines about to give up their faith. Searching and perceptive Christians are becoming refugees in what should be the land of the living, but which rarely offers anything worth living for. When theistism (playing God), buildings, programs, and events replace people, we're losing the path.

In order to reverse our spiritual impoverishment, we need God's help. It is imperative to move in new directions. Our churches ought first to be true communities. People are the priority. Hospitality, love, and forgiveness are to stand out, and our communities should be places of alluring grace. Christian communities are not to be other-worldly, but to be this-worldly. We're to be down-to-earth. We're to share life together. We're to be real people, living in the real world, and doing real things. And Christ is to be Lord of it all—of all life. Others are to come first—through washing feet, laying down lives, loving as Jesus has loved us. This extends to all we say and do as we live in this wild, wonderful, and broken world as broken people. Our actions will never be perfect, but nevertheless we are to continue to seek to demonstrate love in the midst of sin.

Love is never easy, whether it is towards insiders or outsiders, yet we are told that we will be known by our love. This love is deeply connected to living spirituality, as it will result in further transformation into the image of Christ, an empowering for mission, and a diminishing of spiritual impoverishment.

Churches have failed in their obligation to teach relevant, interesting, and insightful map-reading skills. There are more and more Bibles and more and more translations, but we have little encouragement and direction as to how to read the map—this precious word, this Word of God. This is not just a pastor's task, a scholar's task, or seminary student's task, but it is the responsibility of all Christians. We have, generally speaking, become unskilled and illiterate map readers, and this is bound to carry with it grave consequences for our spirituality and our churches.

Many, many times, those who claim to be the most biblical among us are more interested in dogmatically protecting their particular interpretations, rather than carefully studying, contemplating, and being open to the map's direction—a direction they claim to hold so dear. "Whatever the map means to me is what it means" has widespread influence today, and this lack of biblical understanding can and does create serious problems for love and unity. If there is no community, no teaching, and no interest in developing good map-reading skills, then we lose the path and will die. Churches are dying. Tombstones topple steeples. The unreal, impersonal, and dying all too often characterize us. Such a portrayal of Christianity is not accurate, is not of God, is not following the map, is not the path to life, and is certainly not the journey of living spirituality.

True communities will refuse to practice a narrow sectarianism by engaging in a variety of levels of intense map reading and interaction with culture. Exhibiting the imprint of love should be dramatically specific to who we are and what we do. May

God grant us map-reading skills and careful contemplation that leads to renewal, along with cautious and wise participation in our cultures for the sake of creation, for Christ, and for love.

As we seek to follow the map and to be living spirituality, our churches should be made up of those who listen, speak the truth in love, are open to dialogue, and are well informed biblically, spiritually, scientifically, and culturally. Our spirituality is living and to be lived because it is connected to the source and origin of spirituality: Father, Son, and Spirit. This intimate connection provides us with authentic community that can begin to reflect the true community we are to have with each other, and to live out into the world as we seek through the redemption of Christ, in the power of the Spirit, to experience Exodus and bring praise to God.

Destinée Media

Destinée Media publishes both fiction and nonfiction and aims to bring a fresh perspective to spirituality and culture.

At Destinée Media we seek to operate by faith in God within a Biblical/ Christian worldview. We hope to inspire 'culturemaking' by promoting ideas that will contribute to Christ being understood as Lord of the whole of life, which is to be marked by redemption and renewal. We are committed to reflecting carefully on vital matters for the church, academy and society, while aiming to keep a personal and intimate dimension of the Christian life in view.

We thank you for your interest in our materials and hope that you find them both relevant and challenging. Please share your thoughts with us:

www.destineemedia.com

www.ingramcontent.com/pod-product-compliance
Lightning Source LLC
Chambersburg PA
CBHW031252210726
48287CB00003B/1008

* 9 7 8 1 9 3 8 3 6 7 1 3 7 *